Smugglers' tunnel

It was too hot on the beach.
"I'm going in the cave," said Rob.
"It will be cooler in there."

"My dad says there's a secret tunnel in the cave," said Pen. "Smugglers made it to take gold up to the old castle."
"I'm going to find it," said Rob.

"Yes, let's look for it," said Kim.
"Let's find the tunnel," said Trish.

"We might find some gold the smugglers lost," said Sue.
"Yes, and my dad says the person who finds the tunnel wins a prize!" said Rob.

"It's very dark in there!" said Tim.
"Let's just play on the beach."
"No!" shouted the rest of the gang.

"I've got a torch," said Jim.
"I can't get my chair in there,
 but you can take my torch," he said.

"Thanks," said Rob,
"and will you keep Spot here, Jim?
He's afraid of the dark."
Ben said he would stay with Jim, too!

"Fetch Spot, fetch it," called Jim.
"Fetch the stick, Spot," said Ben.

"Look! Look!" shouted Jim.
"Ben, come and see what Spot has found."
"What is it?" said Ben.

"Look, under the rocks and sand! I think it's an old door!" said Jim.

"Pen! Rob! Ali!" yelled Jim. "Quick! Look what Spot has found!"

"It's a door. It's a rusty old door," said Ali.

"Yes," said Jim, "and I bet it leads to the castle!"

"Quick! Open it! Let's see! Quick!" they were all shouting.

The old rusty door creaked and groaned. Slowly, then quickly, very quickly, it came open!

"It's the tunnel! It's the secret smugglers' tunnel! The smugglers hid the door under rocks and sand, but Spot has found it," said Jim. "Clever Spot!" said Rob, proudly patting his little dog.

"Come on! I'm going to see where it goes," shouted Pen.
"Wait, we are coming too," said all the gang.

It was dark.
It was creepy.
It was spooky.

It was very dark, very creepy and *very* spooky!

"What's that?" said the man.
"Where is that banging coming from?"

"Who are you?
Where have you children come from?" he said crossly.

"From the beach! We have found the smugglers' tunnel from the beach!" they all shouted.

"The smugglers' tunnel was lost but you have found it!" said the man.

"The person finding the tunnel wins the prize," said the man. "But it wasn't a person," said Jim, "it was Spot!".

Spot was very proud, and so was Rob, very proud indeed!